A Woman Clothed with the Sun
Did Ancient Prophecy Foretell the Death and Rebirth of American Democracy?
By Jessica DeVoto
Cover Art by Christine Hyman

© 2025 Jessica DeVoto. All rights reserved.
St. Charles, MO
Library of Congress Control Number: 2025913382

Foreword

Although I was baptized Catholic at birth, I wasn't really raised in the Church. I sought and received confirmation in my late teens and was quite fervent for a while, but I no longer identify with the faith and haven't for many years, in part because I believe the Church has lost its way. Today, I consider myself a secular humanist. I believe in loving and caring for my fellow human beings not because it'll get me into heaven or save me from hell but because it's objectively right, and because we all benefit when we all contribute. I believe we can and should answer each other's prayers.

Nonetheless, I can't help but notice striking parallels between ancient eschatological texts and the events unfolding in our own time. In this work, we will explore primarily the Book of Revelation supplemented by selections from the quatrains of Nostradamus and the readings of Edgar Cayce through a secular lens and attempt to uncover what, if anything, they may have foretold about the state of modern American politics. By weaving these texts together, we will explore whether these disparate voices across centuries all saw glimpses of the same destiny unfolding today.

Are these texts describing the end of the world? Or do they offer a cryptic blueprint of our awakening, guiding us to become the saviors we've been waiting for? And if so, how can we save our country and our democracy?

Some may find this exegesis provocative, some might even say blasphemous, because I am discussing American democracy and politics in terms normally reserved for scripture and religious prophecy. To be clear, I am not equating any country, political party, or cause with God or divinity. My intent is not to proselytize but to use the language and symbols of biblical and prophetic texts as a lens through which to better understand the crises of our own time.

In writing this analysis, I did not start with a preconceived conclusion and try to force modern events to fit ancient prophecy. Rather, I began by reading the Book of Revelation, and later, selections from Nostradamus and Cayce, reflecting on the imagery, and considering what real-world events it most closely resembled. After forming those initial interpretations, I sought contemporary journalistic, academic, and other sources to ground those theories.

By exploring these parallels, I hope to illuminate how they might help us recognize and resist authoritarianism, deception, and atrocities in the twenty-first century, as history often rhymes. I invite readers, both religious and secular, to read with an open mind, reflect on the lessons of the past, and ponder what they mean for the crossroads we find ourselves at today.

Chapter 1
A Woman Clothed with the Sun

> "A great sign was seen in heaven: a woman clothed with the sun, and the moon under her feet, and on her head a crown of twelve stars. She was with child. She cried out in pain, laboring to give birth. She gave birth to a son, a male child, who is to rule all the nations with a rod of iron.'" —Revelation 12:1-2,5

This is a powerful image, and an enigmatic one at that. Who or what could this possibly be? Is it a description of Mary giving birth to Jesus? Many theologians believe so, but I always thought that seemed out of place in the Book of Revelation. On September 23rd, 2017, another explanation became apparent when a rare astronomical conjunction occurred[1]. The woman is the constellation Virgo. On this day, the sun was at her shoulder, the moon was at her feet, and the constellation Leo, which has nine bright stars, and three planets, Mercury, Venus, and Mars, were at her head. Jupiter had been in the center of Virgo since November of 2016, roughly the length of a human pregnancy, and on this date, Jupiter exited Virgo to the east, making it look like she was giving birth to it. Jupiter is often referred to as the emperor planet, so in essence, she gave birth to a king-child.

This conjunction, though not unique, is very rare, and it occurred during the first year of Donald Trump's presidency at a time when many were beginning to sense a fundamental shift in America's political and moral direction. Therefore, it gives us a meaningful starting point for our analysis.

Chapter 2
The Rise of Two Beasts

Alongside the woman clothed with the sun, John of Patmos describes a second heavenly sign: an enormous red dragon:

> "Another sign was seen in heaven. Behold, a great red dragon... His tail drew one third of the stars of the sky, and threw them to the earth. The dragon stood before the woman who was about to give birth, so that when she gave birth he might devour her child. She gave birth to a son... Her child was caught up to God and to his throne... The great dragon was thrown down, the old serpent, he who is called the devil and Satan, the deceiver of the whole world. He was thrown down to the earth, and his angels were thrown down with him... The dragon grew angry with the woman, and went away to make war with the rest of her offspring, who keep God's commandments and hold Jesus' testimony." — Revelation 12:3-5,9,17

The constellation Draco lies just below Virgo in the night sky, and as Jupiter exited Virgo in the days following September 23rd, 2017, it appeared to be on a downward trajectory toward Draco until it reversed course and began to rise upwards again, as if being snatched away to avoid being eaten[2].

Once the dragon is hurled to Earth, I believe it transforms into a symbol of the modern-day Republican Party. The Republican Party has long been associated with the color red, and the detail that the dragon swept a third of the stars from the sky may symbolize the 20 states, represented by the stars on the American flag, that voted for Hillary Clinton in the 2016 election[3]. Alternatively, it could refer to the roughly one-third of Republicans who identify as MAGA Republicans and have consistently supported Trump through every scandal, indictment, and authoritarian gesture over the past decade[4].

The war the dragon wages goes beyond politics. It's also the deep divisions that Trump and his followers have sown, turning Americans against one another, waging a war of words, and laying the foundation for a second civil war against the woman's offspring. In this context, I interpret "God's commandments" less as religious dogma and more as America's founding principles of compassion, inclusion, truth, freedom, and justice, which have come under siege in recent years.

After the dragon's descent to Earth, the vision shifts to Earth, where we encounter two symbolic beasts, earthly agents of chaos who bring about America's downfall:

> "...I saw a beast coming up out of the sea... The beast which I saw was like a leopard, and his feet were like those of a bear, and his mouth like the mouth of a lion. The dragon gave him his power, his throne, and great authority. One of his heads looked like it had been wounded fatally. His fatal wound was healed, and the whole earth marveled at the beast... they worshiped the beast, saying, 'Who is like the beast? Who is able to make war with him?' A mouth speaking great things and blasphemy was given to him. Authority to make war for

forty-two months was given to him. He opened his mouth for blasphemy against God, to blaspheme his name, his dwelling, and those who dwell in heaven. It was given to him to make war with the saints and to overcome them. Authority over every tribe, people, language, and nation was given to him." —Revelation 13:1-7

I believe this is a cryptic representation of Donald Trump. It's out of sequence with the great sign discussed in the previous chapter, as Trump had already been in office for several months by the time the conjunction occurred, but one important point to understand about prophecies is that they are symbolic and serve as a lens, so it is very common for events to occur out of sequence or for numbers and other details to be a little off. Rising from the sea may mean he rises from the masses; he was widely known before he entered the political arena. The dragon, i.e. the Republican Party, gave Trump his power and his lofty place in the Oval Office. The fatal wound that healed could be a reference to Trump's first impeachment, his 34 felony convictions, his electoral defeat in 2020, or even his alleged assassination attempt[5,6].

Trump's cult of personality is almost god-like. "Who is like the beast?" echoes the sentiment among his supporters that Trump is incomparable, infallible, or even ordained by God, and one of Trump's favorite statements is, "Nobody knows more about x than me."[7,8] As a narcissist, Trump is extremely prideful and blasphemes truth itself, twisting religion, law, and patriotism to serve his agenda[9]. One need only recall his infamous photo-op at St. John's Church, where he trampled protesters and posed with a Bible[10]. Exactly what a man of faith would do. Not! Moreover, he constantly lambasts America and its citizens for various reasons to aggrandize himself as the only one who can fix it[11].

Of course, he wields extreme power as the president of the United States, not only over Americans but also over the entire world, as America plays an enormous role in global trade and geopolitics. And waging war on the saints, which gets translated as "God's holy people" in some translations, could even refer to the wars going on in Israel[12].

This timeframe of "42 months", "1,260 days", or "time, times, and half a time" appears throughout Revelation. If we use a 360-day prophetic year, as was common in ancient Jewish texts, it aligns closely with the length of a US presidential term. It's as though Revelation offers a coded reference to political power cycles.

Trump served a single term before being defeated by Joe Biden. Just when it seems that the first beast's terror has peaked, a second beast emerges, one even more deceptive, insidious, and dangerous:

> "I saw another beast coming up out of the earth. He had two horns like a lamb and it spoke like a dragon. He exercises all the authority of the first beast in his presence. He makes the earth and those who dwell in it to worship the first beast... He performs great signs, even making fire come down out of the sky to the earth in the sight of people. He deceives my own people who dwell on the earth because of the signs he was granted to do in front of the beast, saying to those who dwell on the earth that they should make an image to the beast... It was given to him to give breath to the image of the beast, that the image of the beast should both speak, and cause as many as

wouldn't worship the image of the beast to be killed. He causes all… to be given marks on their right hands or on their foreheads; and that no one would be able to buy or to sell unless he has that mark, which is the name of the beast or the number of his name… His number is six hundred sixty-six." —Revelation 13:11-18

Yes, this is the infamous 666. Using numerology or other methods to calculate whether someone's name adds up to 666 gets messy quickly and can create a red herring to the true meaning of the passage, so I'm not going to attempt that here. Based on the description, I believe this is Elon Musk. He rises from the earth because he was much less widely-known until he entered politics, and he crept into politics much more subtly. He appears lamb-like because he comes across as soft-spoken and innovative but speaks like a dragon. He deceives the people by claiming to espouse things like free speech, electric vehicles, and "government efficiency", and he performs signs and wonders, like causing fire to come down from heaven, which is likely a reference to programs like SpaceX and Starlink, but increasingly, he uses his power not to innovate but to gain influence, spread disinformation, and amplify Trumpism.

Many believe, as I do, that Musk has become the de facto president, particularly in the early part of Trump's second term, in no small part because he used his extreme wealth and influence to effectively purchase the presidency for Trump[13,14]. Musk props up Trump and Trumpism every chance he gets. A talking image of the beast could refer to Trump's Twitter/X account. Trump was banned from the platform following the January 6th insurrection for spreading disinformation and inciting violence, but then Musk bought out Twitter and immediately reinstated Trump's account[15,16,17].

Now we must ponder the infamous mark of the beast, a passage that has been speculated about for millennia. I always assumed that this would be either some sort of mark on the skin, like a tattoo or a chip, or some kind of payment platform, like PayPal, and no other form of payment would be accepted, or maybe a combination of the two. Although Trump did recently introduce a cryptocurrency called $TRUMP Coin, as of this writing, it has not supplanted the dollar[18]. I suspect this mark is not a literal mark so much as the ideology and actions—the head and the hand, respectively—of embracing Trumpism.

Revelation is not the only prophetic text that may have predicted Trump and Musk. The following quatrain from Nostradamus, the 16th century prophet known for his enigmatic quatrains rife with riddles and layered symbols, tracks eerily well with this interpretation:

> "The false trumpet concealing madness
> Will cause Byzantium to change its laws.
> From Egypt there will go forth a man who wants
> The edict withdrawn, changing money and standards."
> —Century 1, Quatrain 40

It sounds like Nostradamus came close to naming Trump, for another word for trumpet is trump. Concealing madness could be a reference to the business persona that Trump puts on, when in fact, most of Trump's businesses have failed and left a lot of people out of money[19]. Byzantium, later Constantinople and presently Istanbul, was a major cultural and economic center in Nostradamus's time and could be a historic symbol for America[20]. Trump wants to make America change its laws and Constitution to serve himself.

This man from Egypt could be Musk. Musk hails from South Africa, not Egypt, but Nostradamus, being from 16th century Europe, may have lumped Africa as an exotic and faraway land, and again, the location may be symbolic rather than exact. Elon, like Trump, wants to change the laws and Constitution to serve himself and his fellow billionaires. And changing money and standards could be a reference to things like cryptocurrency and Twitter/X.

Chapter 3
The 144,000

Amid the chaos caused by the beasts and their followers, John speaks of a group of 144,000 people who will stand as the resistance.

> "I saw, and behold, the Lamb standing on Mount Zion, and with him a number, one hundred forty-four thousand, having his name and the name of his Father written on their foreheads... They sing a new song before the throne and before the four living creatures and the elders. No one could learn the song except the one hundred forty-four thousand, those who had been redeemed out of the earth. These are those who were not defiled... In their mouth was found no lie, for they are blameless." –Revelation 14:1,3-5

Notably, these 144,000 also bear a seal on their foreheads in stark contrast to the mark of the beast. Again, I don't think this is a literal mark; it's an ideology.

Who might these 144,000 be? Some religious groups, such as Jehovah's Witnesses, interpret this as a literal number of God's elect who will reign with Jesus in heaven while a much larger "great crowd"[21] of devout Christians inherits eternal life on Earth[22]. I don't think this is the case. I believe that number is symbolic; it represents 12,000 from each of the 12 tribes of Israel, meaning that the 144,000 come from all walks of life. I don't think these are necessarily strict religious adherents. In fact, many organized religions have long served the Republican Party and all that it has become[23]. Instead, I believe these are those who refuse to bow to Trump and will fight for democracy, perhaps a subset of which were once Trump supporters but have seen the terrible things he's doing and have joined the resistance. They're truth tellers. They're compassionate. They're awake. They care. They refuse to sit idly by while tyrants burn their country to the ground. They speak out against the lies and deception plaguing our country, that is a new song of truth and hope, even though those that bear the mark of the beast refuse to listen and even though it may put them in danger. This includes truthful journalists, particularly independent journalists like Brian Tyler Cohen[24], whistleblowers like Cassidy Hutchinson[25], activists, teachers and pastors who denounce Trumpism, and most of all, everyday citizens who stand in resistance to authoritarianism even when we're outnumbered. If you're reading this with grief for the loss of the soul of America and a fire in your gut wondering what you can do to get it back, then you are one of them.

Edgar Cayce, a 19th century American seer known as the "Sleeping Prophet", gives us an important reminder:

> "Keep the fires of love burning in thy hearts day by day, for the love of God is manifested in the earth through those that are just kind one to another." —Reading 281-17, Par. 9

Again, if you lead with your compassion and truthfulness, then you are among the 144,000.

Interestingly, the 144,000 are depicted standing on the mountain, and it doesn't say anything about a mark on their hands. This would tend to indicate that they are not taking any major action at this point, or at least, that's the appearance. Their time to act comes later, but for now, they're kind of on the sidelines, perhaps gathering their numbers and contemplating next steps. This echoes what has been going on in Congress and the courts throughout Trump's reign of terror. They have acquitted him on his impeachments, delayed his criminal trials until it was too late, and as yet, done nothing to enforce an order to return an innocent man extrajudicially deported to a foreign gulag, to name just a few instances[26,27,28]. In other words, they have failed to reign Trump in at almost every opportunity, but they'll have their day.

The imagery of the 144,000 standing on the mountain may also evoke the recent wave of protests across the country, particularly the "No Kings" demonstrations on June 14, 2025, held in response to Trump's wasteful and authoritarian birthday parade[29]. People stood on the streets and lifted pro-democracy signs. These protests drew over 13 million participants nationwide, myself included. Not only was this the largest protest in US history, but it also surpassed the 3.5% threshold that scholars often cite as the critical mass necessary to spark nonviolent political change. The number 144,000 could also be a symbolic reference to this rule: 3.5% of 4.1 million. While population estimates from antiquity are imprecise, many historians place the Jewish diaspora around the time Revelation was written between 3 and 6 million[30]. Thus the number 144,000 may represent the portion of the population needed to turn the tide. And in our time, perhaps it already has.

Chapter 4
Another Great Sign

In the same chapter as the 144,000, John of Patmos introduces another figure:

> "I looked, and saw a white cloud, and on the cloud one sitting like a son of man, having on his head a golden crown, and in his hand a sharp sickle. Another angel came out of the temple, crying with a loud voice to him who sat on the cloud, 'Send your sickle and reap, for the hour to reap has come; for the harvest of the earth is ripe!'" –Revelation 14:14-15

This, too, sounds like a sign in the stars, much like the Virgo-Jupiter conjunction. I interpret this as a celestial event involving the constellation Orion and the planet Saturn. Orion appears along the Milky Way, which resembles a cloud, and beginning on November 2nd, 2031, Saturn, renowned for its golden glow, will appear directly above Orion, creating the illusion of a crown upon his head[31]. This event, of course, will occur much later in history than its placement in the Book of Revelation, but for now, we'll file this away as an important date to revisit later.

Chapter 5
The Seven Plagues

Now the tribulation begins in earnest.

> "...I looked, and the temple of the tabernacle of the testimony in heaven was opened. The seven angels who had the seven plagues came out… The temple was filled with smoke from the glory of God and from his power. No one was able to enter into the temple until the seven plagues of the seven angels would be finished." – Revelation 15:5,8

I couldn't imagine what was meant by this imagery until April 21st, 2025 when the death of Pope Francis was announced[32]. The death of a pope is a major event in and of itself, compounded by its timing just after Easter. There is no literal temple currently; I believe this passage may symbolize the papal conclave. Whenever a pope dies, the cardinals assemble in the papal conclave to vote on the next one[33]. During this time, the cardinals are allowed no contact with the outside world, reflecting the detail of no one being able to enter the temple. A two-thirds majority is required to make an election. When all the votes are cast, the ballots are burned, and the smoke is released from the chimney of the Sistine Chapel. Black smoke indicates an inconclusive vote. White smoke tells the world that a successor has been chosen. The candidate can then accept or reject the election.

My initial interpretation was that the temple being filled with smoke might symbolize either a prolonged interregnum, evidenced by black smoke, due to the cardinals disagreeing on whom to elect or the candidate rejecting the election; or the election, with white smoke, of a more puritanical pope, thereby rendering the Church unapproachable for some. Neither of these theories bore out. The Cardinals elected Pope Leo XIV quickly, and he appears, at least for now, to be fairly progressive[34].

Perhaps, then, the smoke in the temple is a reference to the papal conclave itself, not only due to the literal smoke but also because of the solemn mystery and uncertainty surrounding it. Alternatively, it could point to the war in Israel, the land where the Temple once stood[35]. Or maybe the smoke is again symbolic of the disinformation that has clouded global judgment in recent years. In any case, this is a prelude to the coming plagues.

> "The first went, and poured out his bowl into the earth, and it became a harmful and painful sore on the people who had the mark of the beast, and who worshiped his image." –Revelation 16:2

This has been unfolding right before our eyes in the form of an ongoing measles outbreak. Among other things, measles causes disfiguring skin lesions. The measles outbreak started in Texas, a red state, and has been especially prevalent among Republicans–those bearing the mark of the beast–thanks in part to Robert F. Kennedy, Jr. and others dissuading people from vaccinating their children against it despite decades of science indicating that the vaccine is safe and effective[36].

> "The second angel poured out his bowl into the sea, and it became blood as of a dead man. Every living thing in the sea died." —Revelation 16:3

That sounds like a red tide. Red tides are a type of harmful algal bloom that occurs in marine waters when conditions cause Karenia brevis algae to multiply explosively, staining the water a deep red color[37]. This algae is lethal to fin fish, renders shellfish unsafe for consumption, can cause skin irritation, respiratory issues, and neurotoxicity in humans, and can also harm local economies due to unavailability of seafood and decreased tourism. These blooms have been increasing in frequency in recent decades due to climate change and increased runoff from agriculture, wastewater, and urban expansion.

> "The third poured out his bowl into the rivers and springs of water, and they became blood." —Revelation 16:4

This sounds like a harmful algal bloom in freshwater. Just like red tides, these are caused by uncontrolled growth of toxic algae, some of which are red in color, and can cause harm to fish, humans, and drinking water[38]. Again, climate change has increased the frequency of these blooms.

It could also be a reference to water pollution or contaminated drinking water. Flint, Michigan experienced a major water crisis in 2014 due in large part to the water company changing its water source in order to cut costs[39]. This caused skin irritation, increased water main breaks, E. coli and Legionella outbreaks, and lead contamination. And during this time, many residents even reported observing a red discoloration to the water, in keeping with this passage. As the Trump administration guts federal agencies and promotes deregulation of businesses, these incidents will become increasingly difficult to monitor, prevent, and control[40].

> "The fourth poured out his bowl on the sun, and it was given to him to scorch men with fire." —Revelation 16:8

Anyone who hasn't been living under a rock for the last thirty years knows that summers in North America have been getting hotter almost every year. It's gotten to the point that in 2024, Arizona was reportedly having a serious problem with people getting burned on the sidewalks[41].

> "The fifth poured out his bowl on the throne of the beast, and his kingdom was darkened." —Revelation 16:10

This sounds like a major power outage. It specifically says the bowl was poured on the throne of the beast, so this could be localized to the Washington, DC area, or it could affect the entire country and beyond. One possibility is an extreme solar flare. Some scientists and doomsday preppers believe that a rare but intense solar flare could hit the earth some time in 2025[42]. This could disrupt power grids, satellites, telecommunications, and the internet. This effect would be temporary, but it could take weeks or months to recover and cost trillions of dollars. These effects can be mitigated if governments and carriers make the proper preparations. However, with Musk gutting federal agencies and Trump's track record of completely mishandling the COVID-19 pandemic, it seems unlikely they would do so[43].

In fact, Nostradamus may have alluded to the COVID-19 pandemic:

> "Mabus will soon die, then will come,
> A dreadful destruction of people and animals:
> Suddenly vengeance will be revealed,
> Hundreds, hands, thirst and hunger when the comet will pass" —Century 2, Quatrain 62

Mabus could be a reference to George H.W. Bush, who died in 2018[44]. Two years later, the COVID-19 pandemic grips the country and kills over a million Americans[45]. In 2023, the "green comet" C/2022 E3 (ZTF) reached its closest approach to Earth in 50,000 years as the pandemic began to wane[46].

Alternatively, the plague of darkness could simply refer to run-of-the-mill power outages. The US power grid was built in the 1970s and is becoming increasingly outdated and overtaxed[47]. Climate change has caused more extreme weather, the population has grown, and customer needs have changed, all of which has placed increased strain on our power grid, thereby increasing the frequency and duration of outages.

The sixth plague is one of the most esoteric and ominous passages in the entire Book of Revelation:

> "The sixth poured out his bowl on the great river, the Euphrates. Its water was dried up, that the way might be prepared for the kings that come from the sunrise. I saw coming out of the mouth of the dragon, and out of the mouth of the beast, and out of the mouth of the false prophet, three unclean spirits, something like frogs; for they are spirits of demons, performing signs, which go out to the kings of the whole inhabited earth, to gather them together for the war of that great day of God the Almighty… into the place which is called in Hebrew, 'Harmagedon.'" —Revelation 16:12-14,16

There's a lot to unpack here. First, there's the drying up of the River Euphrates. The Euphrates is a real river in modern-day Iraq, but I believe this is used symbolically. In ancient times, the Euphrates would have been an important source of drinking water and a major trade route. Thus this could be a reference to the literal drying up of water sources in the Americas due to climate change. Prolonged drought and increased water demand have caused water levels to drop to historic lows in Lake Mead, the main water source for the western United States, and Gatún Lake, which provides drinking water to half of Panama and feeds the Panama Canal, one of the most vital global trade routes in the world[48,49].

Alternatively or perhaps additionally, it could be a metaphor for Americans' funds drying up due to loss of jobs and government benefits, inflation, and above all, Trump's tariffs. Throughout his second term, Trump has been imposing tariffs in an on-again-off-again pattern on various countries. These taxes on imports serve no real benefit and cost American families thousands of dollars a year, meaning their dollar doesn't stretch as far[50]. They also alienate America from global trade and position Asian countries like China, Japan, and South Korea—kings of the sunrise, or East—as more attractive trade partners[51].

Then we have these three mysterious frog-like demons. What in the world could those be? Again, I believe the dragon, the beast, and the false prophet to represent the Republican Party, Trump, and Musk, respectively, and the detail that they come out of their mouths indicates that it is likely some form of communication, either verbal or written via platforms like Twitter/X and Truth Social. I believe it is simply a strange illustration of deception. Frogs are noisy, but they don't say anything, and they can multiply quickly. Republican elected officials and citizens have long used their microphones and social media to spread disinformation far and wide with ubiquitous devastating consequences. It's one of the biggest problems plaguing America right now. Curiously, a common meme that right wingers use, especially when bullying and gaslighting others, is none other than Pepe the Frog. Kinda makes you wonder.

Why the number three? The number three is a recurring theme in the Bible, but it's not clear in this instance what that refers to. John talks about the frog-demons going out to the kings of the world and gathering them for the final battle. Throughout his two terms, Trump has cozied up to dictators around the world and alienated our allies[52]. Perhaps he will align himself with three major fascist countries, like China, Russia, and North Korea, and there will be a major showdown between that axis and the rest of the world.

John also gives us an important warning in the middle of this plague:

> "Look, I come like a thief! Blessed is the one who stays awake and remains clothed, so as not to go naked and be shamefully exposed." —Revelation 16:15

This is a warning not to fall for the disinformation or turn a blind eye to it. Whenever people say or do things that Republicans disagree with, they often brand us "woke," as if that were an insult, but the descriptor should be worn as a badge of honor because it means you're not sleepwalking off the cliff as so many are; you refuse to snooze the alarm when you see injustice in the world.

Now comes the seventh and final plague:

> "The seventh poured out his bowl into the air... There were lightnings, sounds, and thunders; and there was a great earthquake such as has not happened since there were men on the earth—so great an earthquake and so mighty. The great city was divided into three parts, and the cities of the nations fell... Every island fled away, and the mountains were not found. Great hailstones, about the weight of a talent, came down out of the sky on people." —Revelation 16:17-21

This one is interesting; there are a few ways this could be interpreted. It could be a literal earthquake the likes of which have not been seen in human history, or at least in American history. This could create rifts in the ground that split the country. It could also create tsunamis, which would give the illusion of islands disappearing, and it could even cause mountains to crumble depending on where it occurred.

Another theory is the explosion of the Yellowstone supervolcano. You may or may not know it, but there is an enormous volcano, known as the Yellowstone caldera, underneath the United States right now. The chances of a super eruption in the near future are very low but always possible[53]. If it were to occur, it would have major global impacts, including pyroclastic flows, falling ash (resembling large hail), and temporary climate change.

Still another explanation, and it would be the simplest, is the increasing polarization America is experiencing. The passage says it splits the country in three parts, but America has two main parties: Democrats and Republicans. The third could refer to Independents and Third Parties, emerging rifts within the

Republican Party, or those that don't vote, or it could again just be three as a symbolic number.

Edgar Cayce's predictions seem to rhyme with these verses:

> "As to the changes physical again : The earth will be broken up in the western portion of America. The greater portion of Japan must go into the sea. The upper portion of Europe will be changed as in the twinkling of an eye. Land will appear off the east coast of America. There will be the upheavals in the Arctic and in the Antarctic that will make for the eruption of volcanos in the Torrid areas, and there will be shifting then of the poles…" — Reading 3976-15, Par. 8

The earth being broken up could again be either physical, such as by the Yellowstone supervolcano, or metaphorical in the sense of political polarization. The shifting of the poles sounds like a simultaneous reference to polarization and climate change. Japan going into the sea and Europe changing in the twinkling of an eye are likely allusions to changing trade policy and geopolitical dynamics. Land appearing off the east coast of America might even be a subtle reference to Trump's comments on annexing Greenland[54].

An interesting point about these seven plagues is that Revelation presents them as occurring linearly, presumably with distinctive beginnings and ends, but in our time, they are playing out simultaneously and have been ongoing for quite a while, but what comes next is even scarier.

Chapter 6
The Fall of Babylon

After, or perhaps during, the seven plagues, John of Patmos spends two and a half chapters cryptically describing the fall of a mysterious great city called Babylon:

> "One of the seven angels who had the seven bowls came and spoke with me, saying, 'Come here. I will show you the judgment of the great prostitute who sits on many waters, with whom the kings of the earth committed sexual immorality. Those who dwell in the earth were made drunken with the wine of her sexual immorality.'... I saw a woman sitting on a scarlet-colored beast, full of blasphemous names, having seven heads and ten horns. The woman was dressed in purple and scarlet, and decked with gold and precious stones and pearls, having in her hand a golden cup full of abominations and the impurities of the sexual immorality of the earth. And on her forehead a name was written, 'MYSTERY, BABYLON THE GREAT, THE MOTHER OF THE PROSTITUTES AND OF THE ABOMINATIONS OF THE EARTH.'" —Revelation 17:1-5

I believe Babylon in this context is America. Babylon was an ancient city situated along the Euphrates River. It was a very wealthy city—by some accounts, the world's most splendid city—and was a major hub of commerce and culture, much like Byzantium was in Nostradamus's time and much like America is today[55]. The city in question is described as sitting on many waters. I believe this a symbolic way of saying she has relations with many nations, and perhaps also a comment on the physical breadth of the country, "from sea to shining sea." She's even described as dressed in scarlet and purple, and in a later passage, purple, scarlet, and fine linen, which sounds eerily like red, white, and blue.

I think the references to her adulteries, as well as the gold and precious stones she wears, are an allusion to American consumerism. In the post-World-War-II era, Americans had extraordinary spending power due to plentiful jobs and high wages, and there hadn't been many goods available during the war, as materials were rationed and sent to supply the war effort[56]. This led to a mentality of acquiring more and more goods and having the latest and greatest versions of everything, which was even seen as a patriotic duty. This mentality has persisted over time despite low wages and uncertainty and has helped to prop up the global economy[57]. Obviously, if this pattern were to change drastically, it would spell trouble for the entire world.

John reports being bewildered at the sight of the whore of Babylon:

> "…When I saw her, I wondered with great amazement. The angel said to me, 'Why do you wonder? I will tell you the mystery of the woman and of the beast that carries her… The beast that you saw was, and is not; and is about to come up out of the abyss and to go into destruction. Those who dwell on the earth and whose

names have not been written in the book of life from the foundation of the world will marvel when they see that the beast was, and is not, and shall be present.'" — Revelation 17:6-8

A beast who was, is not, and yet will be present, that's an interesting description. Although the timing is off, I believe this is a reference to Trump serving two nonconsecutive terms as president. Many Trump voters are beginning to regret their vote as his policies tank the economy, cut jobs, kill our standing on the world stage, and create chaos[58]. In other words, they wonder. But to those who have been paying attention, none of this was astonishing in the least. Many of these things are things he campaigned on or did in his first term, and now the entire country and the entire world is suffering the consequences of voter ignorance.

The angel then goes on to tell John of ten kings who have not yet received a kingdom:

> "The ten horns that you saw are ten kings who have received no kingdom as yet, but they receive authority as kings with the beast for one hour. These have one mind, and they give their power and authority to the beast." – Revelation 17:12-13

Who might these ten kings be? My theory is that they are the nine justices of the Supreme Court. The tenth could be Vice President JD Vance, a member of Trump's cabinet, former Attorney General Merrick Garland who was complicit in failing to hold Trump accountable, current attorney general Pam Bondi who will definitely never hold Trump accountable; it could refer to Congress as a whole, who has also all but abdicated their power to Trump, or it could be that it strictly refers to the

Supreme Court justices and the number ten is only symbolic. In any case, it says they give their authority to the beast, which sounds chillingly like the "presidential immunity" ruling that the Supreme Court created out of thin air, which not only rendered the president an effective monarch but also took a huge amount of power away from the Supreme Court[59].

The angel then gives a further description of the beast and his tendencies:

> "The ten horns which you saw, they and the beast will hate the prostitute, will make her desolate, will strip her naked, will eat her flesh, and will burn her utterly with fire." —Revelation 17:16

This aligns perfectly with Trump's unpatriotic attitude and scorched-earth approach to politics[60,61,62]. He is going to his destruction, but unfortunately, he is going to take the entire country down with him, and the world will mourn that loss:

> "The kings of the earth who committed sexual immorality and lived wantonly with her will weep and wail over her, when they look at the smoke of her burning, standing far away for the fear of her torment, saying,'Woe, woe, the great city, Babylon, the strong city! For your judgment has come in one hour.' The merchants of the earth weep and mourn over her, for no one buys their merchandise any more... The fruits which your soul lusted after have been lost to you. All things that were dainty and sumptuous have perished from you, and you will find them no more at all." —Revelation 18:9-11,14

Again, almost every country has benefited from trade relations with America, but now, Trump is straining those relations, which will cause our trade partners to distance themselves from America, and that will have a devastating impact on their economies as well.

America's downfall will be both swift and permanent. The detail about America's doom coming in one hour rings absolutely true, as Trump has destroyed what took generations to build in less than 100 days[63]. America has historically had a reputation as a "shining city upon a hill", a land of freedom and opportunity to be looked up to as a paragon that other nations should strive to achieve. That reputation is gone, and it's unlikely we will ever have it again. Just as many still associate Germany with Hitler, America will forever be the country of Trump. And other countries look on in terror because if fascism can take root in America, it can happen anywhere.

John gives us a stark warning:

> "...Come out of her, my people, that you have no participation in her sins, and that you don't receive of her plagues." —Revelation 18:4

Is this a warning to literally emigrate from America to avoid going down with her? Maybe. For some, that might not be a bad idea. I've considered it myself. The problem is, right-wing extremism is on the rise all over the world[64]. It might be a more metaphorical warning to remove yourself from right-wing news media, like Fox News, right-wing platforms, like Twitter/X, and maybe even relationships with Trump supporters to avoid the disinformation and appearance of guilt by association.

While the world mourns, paradoxically, some find cause to celebrate, seeing an opportunity for a long-overdue reckoning with America's darker legacies:

> "...I heard... a great multitude in heaven, saying, 'Hallelujah! Salvation, power, and glory belong to our God; for his judgments are true and righteous. For he has judged the great prostitute who corrupted the earth with her sexual immorality...'" —Revelation 19:1-2

Despite her reputation as a great nation, America has a lot of faults that far predate the rise of Trump, from our broken healthcare system to systemic racism to exploitation of overseas labor[65,66,67]. Although America as we know it is gone forever, this will give us an opportunity to rebuild in a way that addresses these longstanding issues and for a better country with a better government to rise from the ashes.

Chapter 7
A Heavenly Warrior

Who is it that will rise from the ashes and usher in this new and improved version of America? Revelation gives us some clues:

> "I saw the heaven opened, and behold, a white horse, and he who sat on it is called Faithful and True. In righteousness he judges and makes war. His eyes are a flame of fire, and on his head are many crowns. He has… a name written which no one knows but he himself. He is clothed in a garment sprinkled with blood. His name is called 'The Word of God.' The armies which are in heaven, clothed in white, pure, fine linen, followed him on white horses. Out of his mouth proceeds a sharp, double-edged sword that with it he should strike the nations… He has on his garment and on his thigh a name written, "KING OF KINGS AND LORD OF LORDS."
> —Revelation 19:11-16

Most people read this as a description of Jesus, but I believe this could just as easily represent an earthly figure, the kind of earthly leader America needs for its rebirth.

Although the scripture uses male pronouns, it's entirely plausible that this figure could be a woman or a trans or nonbinary person. In John of Patmos's era, few could imagine such leaders, so he wrote in terms his contemporaries would understand. I, on the other hand, am going to use female pronouns to contrast with the patriarchy of the modern Republican Party, to set her apart from all the presidents before her, and because many of the people who have stood up to Trump to date have been women, including E. Jean Carroll who successfully sued him for defamation, Stormy Daniels who was at the center of his 34 felony convictions, Letitia James who brought the New York financial fraud case barring him from transacting business in the state for three years, Fani Willis who brought his Georgia election interference case, and Kamala Harris who ran against him in the 2024 presidential election[68,69,70].

Edgar Cayce offers us an additional clue:

> "In Russia there comes the hope of the world, not as that sometimes termed of the Communistic, of the Bolshevistic; no. But freedom, freedom! that each man will live for his fellow man! The principle has been born. It will take years for it to be crystallized, but out of Russia comes again the hope of the world. Guided by what? That friendship with the nation that hath even set on its present monetary unit 'In God We Trust.'" — Reading 3976-29, Par 12

This seems ironic, as Russia has been an enemy of freedom throughout history[71]. I believe this is a reference not to Russia proper but rather to Ukraine, a fledgling democracy who has recently come under attack from fascist Russia. Since then, Ukrainian president Volodymyr Zelenskyy has been an exemplary leader, fearlessly standing in the streets of Kyiv alongside his people in defense of their independence[72]. Our heavenly warrior should absolutely take a few pages from Zelenskyy's playbook.

What would this heavenly warrior look like in a modern context? She is described as wearing many crowns yet having a name known only to herself. This would tend to indicate that she is someone who is influential but is as yet not a household name. This could be a cabinet member, the head of a federal agency, an ambassador, a military general, or even the CEO of a large but not mega corporation. These are people whose names usually aren't widely known but who hold a lot of power behind the scenes.

This person would have to be extremely courageous and would need a strong sense of justice, a clear and positive vision for America's future, and above all, an unshakable commitment to truth. It is by the truth alone that the beast will be defeated.

Cayce also emphasized the importance of truth to the freedom of humanity:

> "...Truth by multitudes may be submerged and brought, as it were, to naught, only to rise again and come forth in another individual, or manner, who would assist to bring same, as it were, to light. In the help that is given, there is seen and felt the satisfaction, as of a service rendered to one higher than self..." —Reading 538-16, Par. 4

This leader is that individual. This is evidenced by her as bearing the title "King of Kings and Lord of Lords" on her clothes and her thigh, a detail I interpret not as a claim to divine rulership but as a powerful symbol of her commitment to the rule of law. What governs even the highest elected officials, to which there is no higher earthly authority? The rule of law. Our heavenly warrior is someone who drapes herself with the rule of law, wearing it as a mantle of justice and legitimacy. It is central to her authority, her identity, and her public image, apparently in her words and actions. Unlike Trump, whose motives are rooted in self-interest and aggrandizement, her mission is one of service to truth, justice, and defending democracy.

But we must be careful not to become complacent. Our just leader is strong but not all-powerful; she can't do this single-handedly. Her victory will require an army of ordinary people to amplify her message, uphold the truth, and contribute in any way we can.

Chapter 8
The Final Battle

We've now arrived at the climax of Revelation: the ultimate reckoning between democracy and tyranny, enlightenment and darkness, truth and demagoguery. This is the showdown that will decide America's fate, whether she reclaims her founding principles or gets crushed under the weight of authoritarian rule:

> "I saw the beast, the kings of the earth, and their armies, gathered together to make war against him who sat on the horse and against his army. The beast was taken, and with him the false prophet who worked the signs in his sight, with which he deceived those who had received the mark of the beast and those who worshiped his image. These two were thrown alive into the lake of fire that burns with sulfur. The rest were killed with the sword of him who sat on the horse, the sword which came out of his mouth…
>
> I saw an angel coming down out of heaven, having the key of the abyss and a great chain in his hand. He seized the dragon… and bound him for a thousand years, and cast him into the abyss, and shut it and sealed it over him, that he should deceive the nations no more until the thousand years were finished. After this, he must be freed for a short time." —Revelation 19:19-21, 20:1-3

Trump will wage an outright war on democracy, not with guns and missiles, though that is certainly possible, but rather a battle of ideology through all of Trump's tried and true methods: disinformation, legal manipulation, and attempts to further erode public trust in democracy.

Let us pause for a moment and recall the conjunction of Orion and Saturn we discussed earlier. I believe this is where that comes in. We determined that this will occur on November 2nd, 2031. That is exactly one year before Election Day 2032. Like the Virgo-Jupiter conjunction, this sign in the heavens may not align perfectly with the biblical sequence, but perhaps it marks the period when the final campaign begins in earnest.

Although Trump will have already served two terms as president and therefore should be ineligible to run again in 2028 or 2032, perhaps a Constitutional crisis will allow him to run again or install himself through a legal backdoor, or perhaps another Trump-like candidate will run in his place. Either way, it seems that 2032 will be the year of the final reckoning.

In this election cycle, Trump or his substitute will have the backing of dictators around the world, and they will likely attempt to interfere in the election, but this time, truth will win thanks to our heavenly warrior, whom I will call Nichole, which means "victory of the people"[73], to underscore the idea that this leader's triumph belongs to all who cherish democracy, a victory of the people by the people for the people.

This timing is echoed by Nostradamus:

> "When 20 years of the Moon's reign have passed,
> Another will take up his reign for seven thousand years.

When the exhausted Sun takes up his cycle,
Then my prophecy and threats will be accomplished." —
Century 1, Quatrain 48

The moon's reign could symbolize a period of tribulation and confusion, a Dark Age if you will; whereas the sun taking up its cycle could signify a period of enlightenment. Trump was elected in 2016. Add 20 years, and you land at 2036. Nichole will be elected in 2032, but it will take until 2036 to completely remove Trump's stain. More on that later.

Once inaugurated, Nichole will, at long last, serve justice on Trump and Musk for the harm they've caused our country. Again, they will be defeated by the truth.

John of Patmos states that the beast, Trump, will be bound for 1,000 years. Rather than a literal millennium, I believe this will be 1,000 days, or just short of three years. Trump will go to jail for three years, but for whatever reason, perhaps an appeal or some legal technicality, he will be released for a short time.

Chapter 9
The Final Judgment

During Trump's incarceration, America will enjoy a period of relative peace, but following his release, unsurprisingly, he will go right back to deceiving people and trying to install himself as president again:

> "...After the thousand years, Satan will be released from his prison and he will come out to deceive the nations hich are in the four corners of the earth... to gather them together to the war, whose number is as the sand of the sea. They went up over the width of the earth and surrounded... the beloved city. Fire came down out of heaven from God and devoured them. The devil who deceived them was thrown into the lake of fire and sulfur, where the beast and the false prophet are also. They will be tormented day and night forever and ever."
> –Revelation 20:7-10

Trump will once again rally his supporters and his dictator allies to attack Washington, D.C., the city he both covets and despises as the heart of American democracy, and attempt an insurrection much like the one on January 6th, 2021[74], but this time, they will not succeed; the National Guard will do its job and stop them, arrest them en masse, and prepare them for the final judgment:

> "I saw a great white throne and him who sat on it, from whose face the earth and the heaven fled away. There

was found no place for them. I saw the dead, the great and the small, standing before the throne, and they opened books. Another book was opened, which is the book of life. The dead were judged out of the things which were written in the books, according to their works.... Death and Hades were thrown into the lake of fire. This is the second death.... If anyone was not found written in the book of life, he was cast into the lake of fire." –Revelation 20:11-12,14-15

I believe this is a description of a host of Nuremberg-type trials. John of Patmos calls those that attempted the coup alongside Trump "the dead" because they sold their souls for a lying, hateful tyrant. The books John references I believe symbolize not divine ledgers but rather the rule of law and the Constitution, perhaps also invoking the adage of "throwing the book at them."

Nostradamus invokes book imagery too:

"Those who will have undertaken to subvert,
An unparalleled realm, powerful and invincible:
They will act through deceit, nights three to warn,
When the greatest one will read his Bible at the table."
—Century 5, Quatrain 83

The word Bible comes from the Greek word *biblia*, meaning book[75]. Again, this may not mean the literal Bible but rather the Constitution and the law.

The first death will be their literal punishment: incarceration, deportation, or even execution. The second death will be the eternal stigma of having fought against democracy and being on the wrong side of history. In other words, history will not look kindly on them, nor should it.

Chapter 10
America's Rebirth

Now that Trump and his enablers have been purged once and for all, America will breathe a collective sigh of relief, and America will be made new. John of Patmos gives us a fantastical description of the kind of country those who fight for democracy will inherit:

> "I saw a new heaven and a new earth, for the first heaven and the first earth have passed away, and the sea is no more. I saw the holy city, New Jerusalem, coming down out of heaven from God, prepared like a bride adorned for her husband. I heard a loud voice out of heaven saying, 'Behold, God's dwelling is with people... He will wipe away every tear from their eyes. Death will be no more; neither will there be mourning, nor crying, nor pain any more. The first things have passed away.'
>
> He who sits on the throne said, 'Behold, I am making all things new.' He said, 'Write, for these words of God are faithful and true.' He said to me, "I am the Alpha and the Omega, the Beginning and the End. I will give freely to him who is thirsty from the spring of the water of life. He who overcomes, I will give him these things... But for the cowardly, unbelieving, sinners, abominable, murderers, sexually immoral, sorcerers, idolaters, and all

liars, their part is in the lake that burns with fire and sulfur, which is the second death.'

One of the seven angels who had the seven bowls which were loaded with the seven last plagues… showed me the holy city, Jerusalem, coming down out of heaven from God, having the glory of God. Her light was like a most precious stone, like a jasper stone, clear as crystal; having a great and high wall with twelve gates, and at the gates twelve angels… On the east were three gates, and on the north three gates, and on the south three gates, and on the west three gates. The wall of the city had twelve foundations… The construction of its wall was jasper. The city was pure gold, like pure glass. The foundations of the city's wall were adorned with all kinds of precious stones… The twelve gates were twelve pearls. Each one of the gates was made of one pearl. The street of the city was pure gold, like transparent glass.

I saw no temple in it, for the Lord God the Almighty and the Lamb are its temple… The nations will walk in its light. The kings of the earth bring the glory and honor of the nations into it. Its gates will in no way be shut…, and they shall bring the glory and the honor of the nations into it. There will in no way enter into it anything profane, or one who causes an abomination or a lie, but only those who are written in the Lamb's book of life.

He showed me a river of water of life, clear as crystal, proceeding out of the throne of God and of the Lamb, in the middle of its street. On this side of the river and on that was the tree of life, bearing twelve kinds of fruits, yielding its fruit every month. The leaves of the tree were for the healing of the nations. There will be no curse any more. The throne of God and of the Lamb will be in it, and his servants will serve him. They will see his face, and his name will be on their foreheads… They will reign forever and ever." –Revelation 21:1-14,18-19,21-22,24-27; 22:1-5

Symbolism galore! The old order of things, meaning Trumpism, had passed away, for we did the work to purge it. But we're not going back to the way things were pre-2016; America will have a new birth of freedom and become a better version of herself.

The detail about there no longer being any sea could be interpreted a couple different ways. The sea can be rough, so it could be a symbol of upheaval, and seas create divisions, so it could represent the polarization that has plagued America for so long. Either way, I believe it means that America will finally find peace and safety.

God dwelling among the people, in this context, could be an allegory for democracy itself, that we will have a just leader like Nichole who listens to her constituents and does everything in her power to make America the best it can be for ordinary people, not billionaires and lobbyists. Her throne is in the city so that she is accessible to her constituents, and her servants serve her, meaning that they understand and execute their civic duties. The detail of no temple in the city I believe symbolizes not that there would be literally no religion in the country and thus no places of worship but rather that we would see a return to a healthy separation of church and state. No more death or suffering obviously is not possible in a literal sense, but it could mean that we will have better healthcare and social safety nets to keep people from dying of preventable diseases, starvation, exposure, or violence. The river flowing down the middle of the city with the tree of life on both sides bearing various fruits every month is an illustration of equity. Everyone has access to the basic necessities of life, and resources are no longer hoarded by few ultrarich robber barons. The golden streets could be representative of a country that invests in its infrastructure and that shares its wealth. I'm not talking about socialism; I simply mean a system that doesn't make it easy for a few privileged individuals to hold the vast majority of the wealth.

The jasper walls and pearly gates could be a symbol of a country that has secure borders but that welcomes travelers and immigrants seeking freedom. The foundations made of precious stones likely represent democratic principles: liberty, justice, truth, bravery, equity, compassion, and the rule of law, to name a few. The gates are made of pearl, not iron; they're beautiful, not brutal, and there are gates on all four sides, meaning that they are open to people from all over the world, not just a few favored countries. In this new America, we will finally embody the spirit captured by Emma Lazarus on the pedestal of the Statue of Liberty:

> "Give me your tired, your poor, Your huddled masses yearning to breathe free, The wretched refuse of your teeming shore. Send these, the homeless, tempest-tost to me. I lift my lamp beside the Golden Door!"

The statement "I am the Alpha and the Omega" may sound antithetical to a democratic leader, but I believe it's better interpreted as "I represent the Alpha and the Omega," meaning she works for the people from all walks of life, from the richest of the rich to the poorest of the poor. The people wearing her name on their foreheads could symbolize a return to patriotism–not nationalism, which helped cause America's downfall–but true patriotism, being proud, in the best way possible, to be an American. By the time these events play out, the 2036 election would probably be around the corner, underway, or just passed, so this entire chapter and a half of Revelation almost reads like a campaign or inauguration speech for Nichole's second term. Again, she is committed to truth and transparency. She will see that America becomes this earthly paradise and stays that way.

With these reforms, Nichole will lay the foundation for a new American age, one that, if we're vigilant, could endure far longer than any democracy in history. Perhaps this is the dawn of the "seven thousand years" Nostradamus envisioned: not a literal time frame but a long and lasting age of enlightenment.

Don't get me wrong. No country, government, or leader will ever be perfect or without corruption but Nichole will continually strive for a more perfect union. She might amend or even rewrite the Constitution to enshrine safeguards against authoritarianism and demagoguery, to ensure that no new Trump ever comes near the levers of power again.

Afterword

We have journeyed through the apocalyptic visions of Revelation, the cryptic quatrains of Nostradamus, and the psychic insights of Edgar Cayce, not to predict a far-off cataclysm, but to comprehend the the very real and very urgent political, moral, and existential crises we find ourselves in today.

Through these symbols, patterns, and prophecies, a message emerges: our future is not set in stone. Although the warning signs seem Biblical, the outcome is ours to shape. We can make things right. Prophecy demands not resignation but discernment. It challenges us to stay awake and vigilant, to recognize the signs, and to take action and to act with courage and compassion.

The fall of Babylon, the defeat of the beast, and the rise of a just new order are already unfolding at the ballot box and in the courts, in classrooms and in protests, in online discourse and in private conversations. It's not simply about Trump or Musk or any single demagogue; it's about what kind of country we want to be and what we are willing to do to become it.

We must be the 144,000, not in number but in spirit. We must show up, speak out, tell the truth, and defend what's right, even when it's unpopular or unsafe. We are the resistance, and we are the savior we've been waiting for.

If we want a leader like Nichole, then we must create the conditions for her (or him or them) to arise, and we must support that leader not with blind fealty but with clarity, vigilance, and hope. Maybe she could even be you.

This book is not meant to be scary, although the stakes are terrifying; it is meant to illuminate and to empower. It is a reminder that darkness always overreaches, but that the light, though it may flicker, never dies. Even a small candle can pierce the night.

This is not the end; it is the beginning of something new. Let's build it together!

References

[1] Reagan, David. "Investigating the Great Sign of Revelation 12." *Christ in Prophecy Blog*, 30 Aug. 2017, https://christinprophecyblog.org/2017/08/investigating-the-great-sign-of-revelation-12/.

[2] Stellarium. Stellarium Team, https://stellarium-web.org/. Accessed 21 April 2025.

[3] Electoral Ventures LLC. "2016 Presidential Election." *270 To Win*, 2025, https://www.270towin.com/2016-election.

[4] Selcher, Wayne A. "A Profile of Trump Voters: The Demographics of His MAGA Enthusiasts and Their Relationship to Him." *Observatorio Politico dos Estados Unidos*, 18 Sept. 2024, https://www.270towin.com/2016-election.

[5] Sisak, Michael R., et al. "Guilty: Trump Becomes First Former US President Convicted of Felony Crimes." *Associated Press*, 31 May 2024, https://apnews.com/article/trump-trial-deliberations-jury-testimony-verdict-85558c6d08efb434d05b694364470aa0.

[6] ABC News. "Video Shows Moment of Trump Assassination Attempt at Rally." *YouTube*, July 2024, https://youtu.be/LAk6dXEzIUo?si=_rWtysTjPYYhi_Zu.

[7] Maqbool, Aleem. "'Anointed by God': The Christian Who See Trump as Their Saviour." *BBC*, 16 Nov. 2024, https://www.bbc.com/news/articles/c20g1zvgj4do.

⁸ NowThis Impact. "'Nobody Knows More' Than Trump About Anything: A Supercut." *YouTube*, 2020, https://youtu.be/sR3f95BGIiA?si=v25xJIjmGB_CtmC5.

⁹ Kimmins, Leigh. "Trump Brags About How Much Fun He's Having Running 'The World'." *The Daily Beast*, 28 April 2025, https://www.thedailybeast.com/trump-brags-about-how-much-fun-hes-having-running-the-world/.

¹⁰ Horsley, Scott. "Trump's Unannounced Church Visit Angers Church Officials." *NPR*, 1 June 2020, https://www.npr.org/2020/06/01/867532070/trumps-unannounced-church-visit-angers-church-officials.

¹¹ Today. "Donald Trump's Dark, Fiery Speech: 'I Alone Can Fix' America. *YouTube*, 2017, https://youtu.be/8pnmMxbEjdc?si=Vp4ZrlTGR25wjvsh.

¹² "What Is Hamas and Why Is It Fighting with Israel in Gaza?" *BBC News*, 21 Jan. 2025, https://www.bbc.com/news/world-middle-east-67039975.amp.

¹³ Dier, Arden. "Musk Is Now the 'De Facto President'." *Newser*, 12 Feb. 2025, https://www.yahoo.com/news/buying-presidency-elon-musk-spent-145334497.html.

¹⁴ Davis, Charles R. "Buying a Presidency: Elon Musk Spent Over $250 Million to Elect Donald Trump." *Yahoo News*, 6 Dec. 2024, https://www.yahoo.com/news/buying-presidency-elon-musk-spent-145334497.html.

¹⁵ Allyn, Bobby, and Tamara Keith. "Twitter Permanently Suspends Trump, Citing 'Risk of Further Incitement of Violence.'" *NPR*, 8 Jan. 2021, https://www.npr.org/2021/01/08/954760928/twitter-bans-president-trump-citing-risk-of-further-incitement-of-violence.

¹⁶ Pequeño IV, Antonio. "Elon Musk Says xAI Has Purchased X, Formerly Known as Twitter, for $33 Billion." *Forbes*, 28 Mar. 2025,

https://www.forbes.com/sites/antoniopequenoiv/2025/03/28/elon-musk-says-xai-has-purchased-x-formerly-known-as-twitter-for-33-billion/.

[17] "Elon Musk Says He's Reinstating Donald Trump's Twitter Account." *CBS News*, 20 Nov. 2022, https://www.cbsnews.com/amp/news/elon-musk-says-donald-trump-reinstated-twitter/.

[18] Roush, Tyler. "Donald Trump Launches 'TRUMP' Meme Coin; Token Exceeds $1.2 Billion Market Cap." *Forbes*, 19 Jan. 2025, https://www.forbes.com/sites/tylerroush/2025/01/19/donald-trump-launches-trump-meme-coin-token-exceeds-12-billion-market-cap/.

[19] Pod Save America. "Ranking Donald Trump's WORST Business Failures." *YouTube*, 2024, https://youtu.be/O8s1kaNkGLA?si=FDNP0MZM2BVyQ2Xa.

[20] Hendrix, David. "Constantinople and the Byzantine Legacy." *The Byzantine Legacy*, 2016, https://www.thebyzantinelegacy.com/.

[21] Revelation 7:9

[22] "Who Goes to Heaven?" *JW.org*, Watch Tower Bible and Tract Society of Pennsylvania, https://www.jw.org/en/bible-teachings/questions/go-to-heaven/.

[23] Smith, Peter. "White Evangelical Voters Show Steadfast Support For Donald Trump's Presidency." *Associated Press*, 7 Nov. 2024, https://apnews.com/article/dbfd2b4fe5b2ea27968876f19ee20c84.

[24] Cohen, Brian Tyler. Brian Tyler Cohen. *YouTube*, https://www.youtube.com/c/BrianTylerCohen. Accessed 23 April 2025.

[25] Fox 5 Atlanta. January 6 Hearing: Trump Aide Cassidy Hutchinson Full Testimony. *YouTube*, 28 June 2022, www.youtube.com/live/yShPW0Gl914?si=KQH_3KnFxVyhkMzH.

[26] Montanaro, Domenico. "Senate Acquits Trump in Impeachment Trial–Again." *NPR*, 13 Feb. 2021, https://www.npr.org/sections/trump-impeachment-trial-live-updates/2021/02/13/967098840/senate-acquits-trump-in-impeachment-trial-again.

[27] Truax, Chris. "A Monument to Failure: Jack Smith's Report and What Might Have Been." *The Hill*, 17 Jan. 2025, https://thehill.com/opinion/judiciary/5089488-trump-jack-smith-report-failure/amp/.

[28] Zirin, James D. "If Trump Flouts the Abrego Garcia Rulings, The Constitution Is Done." *The Hill*, 22 April 2025, https://thehill.com/opinion/judiciary/5259208-if-trump-flouts-the-abrego-garcia-rulings-the-constitution-is-done/.

[29] Tietz, Dani. "Millions Take to Streets in Historic 'No Kings' Protests Across United States." *Mahomet Daily*, 16 June 2025, https://mahometdaily.com/millions-take-to-streets-in-historic-no-kings-protests-across-united-states/.

[30] "Early Jewish Diaspora: 600 B.C. to 500 A.D." *Africame: Facts and Details*, Accessed 17 June 2025, https://africame.factsanddetails.com/article/entry-648.html.

[31] Stellarium. Stellarium Team, https://stellarium-web.org/. Accessed 23 April 2025.

[32] Watkins, Devon. "Pope Francis Has Died on Easter Monday Aged 88." *Vatican News*, 21 April 2025, https://www.vaticannews.va/en/pope/news/2025-04/pope-francis-dies-on-easter-monday-aged-88.html.

[33] Natanson, Phoebe and Christopher Watson. "Electing a New Pope: What Happens Next and What Is a Papal Conclave?" *ABC News*, 21 April 2025, https://abcnews.go.com/International/electing-new-pope-after-francis-death/story?id=107589579.

[34] Kim, Juliana and Ayana Archie. "Who Is the New Pope Leo XIV and What Is His Background?" *NPR*, 17 June 2025, https://www.npr.org/2025/05/08/g-s1-65147/new-pope-leo-xiv-robert-prevost-views

[35] Walsh, Joe, et al. "Iran Launches Missiles at Isarael, and Some Hit Tel Aviv, as Israel Attacks Iranian Nuclear Sites and Commanders." CBS

News, 14 June 2025, https://www.cbsnews.com/news/iran-israel-drone-attack-retaliation-strikes-on-nuclear-sites-and-commanders/.

[36] Godoy, Maria. "Amid a Growing Measles Outbreak, Doctors Worry RFK Jr. Is Sending the Wrong Message." *NPR*, 7 March 2025, https://www.npr.org/2025/03/07/nx-s1-5320352/measles-rfk-west-texas-outbreak.

[37] "What Is Red Tide?" *WEDU PBS*, 1 Aug. 2023, https://www.wedu.org/blogs/sustain/red-tide/.

[38] Denchak, Melissa. "Freshwater Harmful Algal Blooms 101." *Natural Resources Defense Council*, 28 Mar. 2024, https://www.nrdc.org/stories/freshwater-harmful-algal-blooms-101.

[39] Masten, Susan J, Simon H Davies, Shawn P McElmurry. "Flint Water Crisis: What Happened and Why?" *Journal - American Water Works Association*, vol. 108, no. 12 (2016), pp. 22-34. Retrieved from https://pmc.ncbi.nlm.nih.gov/articles/PMC5353852/.

[40] "Musk's DOGE Cuts Cripple Government Agencies for a Fraction of Promised Savings." *NARFE*, 22 Apr. 2025, https://www.narfe.org/blog/2025/04/22/musks-doge-cuts-cripple-government-agencies-for-a-fraction-of-promised-savings/.

[41] Hassan, Adeel and Isabelle Taft. "Burns From Scorching-Hot Sidewalks and Roads Are Rising, and Can Be Fatal." *The New York Times*, 14 July 2024, https://www.nytimes.com/2024/07/14/us/heat-wave-pavement-burns.html.

[42] The Washington Post Editorial Board. "The Next Global Crisis Could Come from the Sun. We Should Prepare Now." *The Washington Post*, 7 May 2024, https://www.washingtonpost.com/opinions/interactive/2024/solar-storm-threat-electric-grid/.

[43] Charen, Mona. "Don't Forget How Trump Mishandled the Pandemic." *Chicago Sun-Times*, 7 June 2024, https://chicago.suntimes.com/columnists/2024/06/07/donald-trump-covid-

pandemic-quack-cures-masking-vaccination-republican-death-rates-mona-charen.

[44] NBC News. "President George H.W. Bush Dies at 94." *YouTube*, 2019, https://youtu.be/aq6-Ta-BlTQ?si=a00QnjuBHL3xdpOt.

[45] Johnson, Carla K. "US Deaths from COVID Hit 1 Million, Less Than 2 ½ Years In." *AP News*, 16 May 2022, https://apnews.com/article/us-covid-death-toll-one-million-7cefbd8c3185fd970fd073386e442317.

[46] Kluger, Jeffrey. "The Story Behind a Once-in-a-Lifetime Green Comet That's About to Fly Past Earth." *Time*, 31 Jan. 2023, https://time.com/6251170/green-comet-2023-story-behind/#.

[47] "Why the US Power Grid Has Become Unreliable." *CNBC*, 12 Aug. 2022, https://www.cnbc.com/video/2022/08/12/why-the-us-power-grid-has-become-unreliable.html.

[48] "Is Lake Mead Drying Up? Reservoir Reaches Historic Low." *Planning and Conservation League*, 15 June 2022, https://pcl.org/is-lake-mead-drying-up-reservoir-reaches-historic-low/.

[49] Ruiz, Sarah and Christina Shintani. "Drought in Panama Is Disrupting Global Shipping. These 7 Graphics Show How." *Woodwell Climate Research Center*, 20 Feb. 2024, https://www.woodwellclimate.org/drought-panama-canal-7-graphics/.

[50] Yu, Yi-Jin. "Trump's Tariffs: How American Families, Parents Will Be Impacted." *ABC News*, 7 April 2025, https://abcnews.go.com/amp/GMA/Family/trumps-tariffs-american-families-parents-impacted/story?id=120561710.

[51] Schuman, Michael. "Trade Will Move On Without the United States." *The Atlantic*, 7 April 2025, https://www.theatlantic.com/international/archive/2025/04/trump-tariffs-hegemony-decline/682323/.

[52] Amanpour and Company. "CNN: Rep. Moulton Reacts to Trump's Speech to Congress: 'It Doesn't Make Sense'." *YouTube*, Accessed 24 April 2025, https://youtu.be/f3u1fipq_-4?si=i8FafCWUHiahjVg4.

[53] "What Would Happen If a 'Supervolcano' Eruption Occurred Again at Yellowstone?" *United States Geographic Survey*, 7 Nov. 2024, https://www.usgs.gov/faqs/what-would-happen-if-a-supervolcano-eruption-occurred-again-yellowstone.

[54] Times News. "Donald Trump Vows to Annex Greenland." *YouTube*, March 2025, https://youtu.be/bwFQEO4D9VY?si=yGTQarg9oaq7qPQv.

[55] Saggs, Henry W.F. "Babylon." *Encyclopedia Britannica*, 22 Apr. 2025, https://www.britannica.com/place/Babylon-ancient-city-Mesopotamia-Asia.

[56] "The Rise Of American Consumerism." *PBS*, Accessed 25 April 2025, https://www.pbs.org/wgbh/americanexperience/features/tupperware-consumer/.

[57] Chon, Gina and Pete Sweeney. "Global Economy Can Thank U.S. Consumers." *Reuters*, 30 August 2022, https://www.reuters.com/breakingviews/global-economy-can-thank-us-consumers-2022-08-30/.

[58] Sloss, Morgan. "'WHY ARE PEOPLE SO STUPID': This MAGA Supporter Shared 10 Reasons Why They Regret Voting for Trump, and the Internet Is Not Impressed." *Yahoo News*, 9 April 2025, https://www.yahoo.com/news/trump-supporter-listed-10-reasons-204247507.html.

[59] Brian Tyler Cohen. "Supreme Court Ruling Suddenly Endangers EVERY Trump Prosecution." *YouTube*, 2024, https://youtu.be/ZoNKFC8P9hI.

[60] "Trump's Dystopian View of America." *PBS*, 13 Sept. 2024, https://www.pbs.org/weta/washingtonweek/video/2024/09/trumps-dystopian-view-of-america.

[61] Goldberg, Jeffrey. "Trump: Americans Who Died in Ware Are 'Losers' and 'Suckers'." *The Atlantic*, 3 Sept. 2020, https://www.theatlantic.com/politics/archive/2020/09/trump-americans-who-died-at-war-are-losers-and-suckers/615997/.

[62] Benen, Steve. "Lara Trump Touts 'Scorched Earth' Agenda After 2024 Elections." *MSNBC*, 22 April 2024, https://www.msnbc.com/msnbc/amp/shows/maddow/blog/rcna148790

[63] McManus, Allison, et al. "100 Days of the Trump Administration's Foreign Policy: Global Chaos, American Weakness, and Human Suffering." *Center For American Progress*, 24 April 2025, https://www.americanprogress.org/article/100-days-of-the-trump-administrations-foreign-policy-global-chaos-american-weakness-and-human-suffering/.

[64] Allchorn, William. "Understanding Global Right-Wing Extremism." *Lowy Institute*, 12 Sept. 2022, https://www.lowyinstitute.org/the-interpreter/understanding-global-right-wing-extremism.

[65] Asare, Janice Gassam. "How the American Healthcare System Is Failing Its People." *Forbes*, 7 Dec. 2024, https://www.forbes.com/sites/janicegassam/2024/12/07/how-the-american-healthcare-system-is-failing-its-people/.

[66] Smith, Robert. "Key Examples of Systemic Racism in the U.S." *Robert Smith*, 24 August 2023, https://robertsmith.com/blog/examples-of-systemic-racism/.

[67] Zimmerman, Cathy, et al. "Addressing Labour Exploitation in the Global Workforce." *The Lancet*, vol. 403, no. 10438, 4 May 2024, pp. 1748. Retrieved from https://www.thelancet.com/journals/lancet/article/PIIS0140-6736(24)00459-8/fulltext.

[68] Bustillo, Ximena. "Jury Orders Trump to Pay $83 Million for Defaming Columnist E. Jean Carroll." *NPR*, 26 Jan. 2024, https://www.npr.org/2024/01/26/1226626397/trump-defamation-trial

[69] Tawfik, Nada. "Donald Trump Hit Where It Hurts Most in New York Fraud Ruling." *BBC News*, 17 Feb. 2024, https://www.bbc.com/news/world-us-canada-68323086.amp.

[70] Ginglas, Sam. "Atlanta DA Willis Begins Her Second Term Expressing No Regrets Over Trump Case." *NPR*, 25 Feb. 2025,

https://www.npr.org/2025/02/24/nx-s1-5302917/fani-willis-president-trump-georgia-case.

[71] Lipman, Maria. "How Russia Has Come to Loathe the West." *European Council on Foreign Relations*, 15 March 2015, https://ecfr.eu/article/commentary_how_russia_has_come_to_loathe_the_west311346/?amp.

[72] The Sun. "'We Are Still Here' Says Defiant Ukraine President Zelenskyy on Streets of Kyiv, 2022, https://youtu.be/Pa7fXDy5Gdg?si=7wmSD_3oksFvaE9f.

[73] Moss, Jennifer. "Nichole." *BabyNames.com*, 30 April 2025, https://babynames.com/name/Nichole.

[74] "The January 6 Attack on the U.S. Capitol." *American Oversight*, 26 Sept. 2023, https://americanoversight.org/investigation/the-january-6-attack-on-the-u-s-capitol/.

[75] "Origin and History of *Bible*." *Online Etymology Dictionary*, Accessed 28 April 2025, https://www.etymonline.com/word/Bible.

All Bible quotes retrieved from BibleGateway.com, World English Bible translation.

All Nostradamus quotes retrieved from https://www.crystalinks.com/quatrains.html.

All Cayce quotes retrieved from Association for Research and Enlightenment.

www.ingramcontent.com/pod-product-compliance
Lightning Source LLC
Chambersburg PA
CBHW020520030426
42337CB00011B/488